Temecula Quilt Co.

Returning to Temecula

SCRAPPY QUILTS WITH A NOD TO THE PAST

Sheryl Johnson

Martingale
Create with Confidence

Temecula Quilt Co.
Returning to Temecula: Scrappy Quilts with a Nod to the Past
© 2019 by Sheryl Johnson

Martingale®
19021 120th Ave. NE, Ste. 102
Bothell, WA 98011-9511 USA
ShopMartingale.com

Printed in China
24 23 22 21 20 19   8 7 6 5 4 3 2 1

Library of Congress Cataloging-in-Publication Data is available upon request.

ISBN: 978-1-68356-021-0

MISSION STATEMENT

We empower makers who use fabric and yarn to make life more enjoyable.

CREDITS

PUBLISHER AND
CHIEF VISIONARY OFFICER
Jennifer Erbe Keltner

CONTENT DIRECTOR
Karen Costello Soltys

DESIGN MANAGER
Adrienne Smitke

MANAGING EDITOR
Tina Cook

PRODUCTION MANAGER
Regina Girard

ACQUISITIONS EDITOR
Laurie Baker

COVER DESIGNER
Mia Mar

TECHNICAL EDITOR
Nancy Mahoney

BOOK DESIGNER
Missy Shepler

COPY EDITOR
Jennifer Hornsby

LOCATION PHOTOGRAPHER
Adam Albright

STUDIO PHOTOGRAPHER
Brent Kane

ILLUSTRATOR
Sandy Loi

SPECIAL THANKS
Photography for this book was taken at the Garden Barn in Indianola, Iowa (TheGardenBarn.com).

Contents

#temeculaquiltco

CORD COTTON FOR HAND AND MACHINE

J. & P. COATS

WARRANTED
150 YARDS

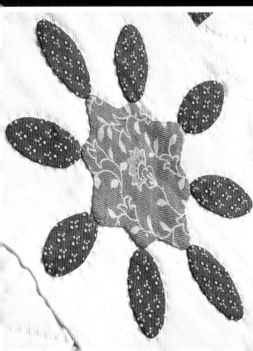

Introduction

My first book, *Quirky Little Quilts*, was published in 2018 by Martingale. It celebrated quilts with unconventional characteristics and irregular traits. I'm thrilled to have the opportunity to bring you variations on that theme with the publication of my second book, *Returning to Temecula*. Let's take a closer look at what makes this quirky style of quilting so enduring and endearing. Quirky is defined as unconventional, uncommon, irregular, and extraordinary. The quiltmakers of the past used what they had, and as a result, they created quilts with a wonderful make-do quality and sometimes a slightly asymmetrical or off-kilter look. It is these quirky little surprises that make small vintage quilts so appealing to me.

You can up your quirky quotient as you select fabric, assemble blocks, and put the finishing touches on your quilts. Take a closer look at Timeless Traditions (page 11). Notice anything? I ran out of the bright blue fabric I had originally selected for sashing and borders, but no problem. With a little substitution of a similar color print, I was back in business.

Add to the uniqueness of your quilts by mixing things up a bit. Sixteen Squares (page 7) has four-patch units that match, and some that are purposely mismatched, to give it the uncommon and irregular look that I love. Little Leftovers (page 71) is the perfect example of a slightly odd and perfectly extraordinary little quilt. It has a collected-over-time appeal; the leftover blocks that once filled a quiltmaker's sewing basket have been given a new purpose.

Little quilts, especially quirky ones, add charm and character to any room in your home. Look for interesting containers, baskets, and boxes to fill with your tiny treasures. Take a fresh look at the vintage treasures in your home for a new way to show off your one-of-a-kind creations. Continue to find inspiration and share in all the happenings of Temecula Quilt Co. on Instagram, Facebook, and Pinterest @temeculaquiltco, or on our blog, temeculaquiltco.blogspot.com. And post any of the patterns you make with the hashtag #temeculaquiltco.

We are so happy to have you along!

—*Sheryl Johnson*

Sixteen Squares

PIECED AND HAND QUILTED BY SHERYL JOHNSON

A Sixteen Patch quilt by an unknown 1890s maker was the inspiration for my reproduction. I love all the colorful tidbits of fabric that come together to create this simple little project. Pay close attention to color placement to ensure that the medallion will be the center of attention. Construct the encircling four-patch units from a wonderful variety of your special scraps. All those pieces of fabric that you can't quite part with are sure to make this quilt a treasured favorite. Counting to 16 has never been so much fun.

Materials

Yardage is based on 42"-wide fabric.

⅝ yard *total* of assorted light, medium, and dark prints in reds, blues, browns, creams, pinks, greens, blacks, and golds for blocks

⅛ yard of light print for border

⅛ yard of brown print for binding

⅝ yard of fabric for backing

22" × 22" piece of cream flannel or batting

Cutting

Refer to the quilt photo and the assembly diagram on page 9 for fabric and color inspiration for the Sixteen Patch blocks.

From the assorted light, medium, and dark prints, cut:

- 136 pairs of matching squares, 1⅜" × 1⅜" (272 total)

From each of 1 red, 1 brown, and 1 blue print, cut:

- 8 squares, 1⅜" × 1⅜" (24 total)

From each of 3 assorted light prints, cut:

- 8 squares, 1⅜" × 1⅜" (24 total)

From the light print for border, cut:

- 2 strips, 2¼" × 11"
- 2 strips, 2¼" × 7½"

From the brown print for binding, cut:

- 2 strips, 1½" × 42"

Making the Blocks

Press all seam allowances as indicated by the arrows.

1 Lay out two pairs of 1⅜" squares in two rows. Join the squares to make a four-patch unit measuring 2¼" square, including seam allowances. Make 68 units.

Make 68 units,
2¼" × 2¼".

2 Lay out four units in two rows of two. Join the units to make a Sixteen Patch block measuring 4" square, including seam allowances. Make 16 scrappy blocks. Repeat to make one Sixteen Patch block using four brown four-patch units.

Make 16 blocks,   Make 1 block,
4" × 4".   4" × 4".

3 Lay out eight matching red 1⅜" squares and eight matching light squares in four rows of four. Sew the squares together in rows. Join the rows to make a center block measuring 4" square, including seam allowances. Repeat to make one center block using eight matching brown squares and eight matching light squares. Make one center block using eight matching blue squares and eight matching light squares.

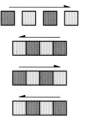

Make 3 two-color blocks,
4" × 4".

Assembling the Quilt Top

1 Lay out the three center blocks and the brown Sixteen Patch block in two rows of two. Sew the blocks together into rows. Join the rows to make the center medallion, which should measure 7½" square, including seam allowances.

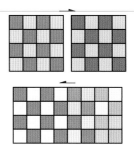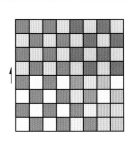

Make 1 section,
7½" × 7½".

2 Sew the light 2¼" × 7½" strips to the top and bottom of the center medallion and the light 2¼" × 11" strips to the sides of the medallion. The quilt center should measure 11" square, including seam allowances.

3 Join three Sixteen Patch blocks to make the left border. Repeat to make the right border. These borders should measure 4" × 11", including seam allowances.

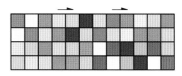

Make 2 side borders,
4" × 11".

4 Join five Sixteen Patch blocks to make the top border. Repeat to make the bottom border. The borders should measure 4" × 18", including seam allowances.

Make 2 top/bottom borders,
4" × 18".

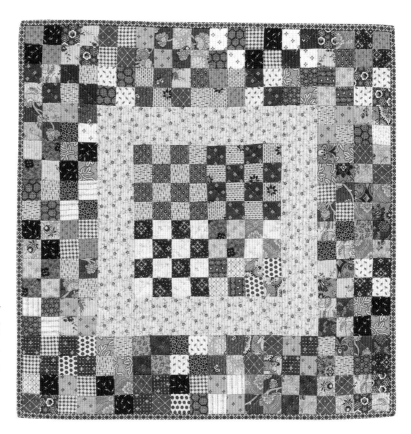

Notice how the light-colored inner border **FOCUSES ATTENTION** *on the four-block center medallion.*

5 Sew the side borders to the left and right edges of the quilt center. Add the top and bottom borders to complete the quilt top. The quilt top should measure 18" square.

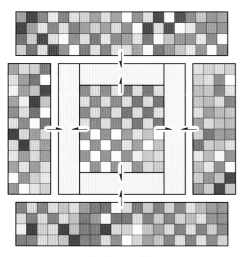

Quilt assembly

Finishing the Quilt

For detailed information about any finishing steps, visit ShopMartingale.com/HowtoQuilt.

1 Layer the quilt top, flannel or batting, and backing; baste the layers together using your preferred method.

2 Quilt by hand or machine. Sixteen Squares is hand quilted in a diagonal crosshatch pattern through the center of each block.

3 Using the brown 1½"-wide strips, make single-fold binding (page 77) and then attach the binding to the quilt.

4 Make a label using a small piece of muslin, being sure to include your name and the date. Turn under the edges and hand stitch the label to the back of your quilt.

Timeless Traditions

PIECED BY SHERYL JOHNSON AND MACHINE QUILTED BY DEBBIE BLAIR

Graphic hourglass units surrounding the traditional Oak Leaf appliqué block give this vintage redo a timeless appeal. The neutral-colored blocks create the perfect understated backdrop against which the colorful medallion center can really shine. The finishing touch that guarantees this project will become an instant classic is what I like most: the unexpected use of cobalt blue sashing.

Materials

Yardage is based on 42"-wide fabric. Fat eighths measure 9" x 21". Fat quarters measure 18" x 21".

1 fat eighth of green print for center medallion appliqué

4" × 8" rectangle of red print for center medallion appliqué

1 fat quarter of cream solid for center medallion background

⅓ yard *total* of assorted brown and gray prints for hourglass units (collectively referred to as "brown")

⅓ yard *total* of assorted light prints for hourglass units

⅓ yard of taupe print for setting squares and outer border

¼ yard of blue print A for sashing and inner border

¼ yard of blue print B for binding

⅞ yard of fabric for backing

31" × 31" piece of batting

Cutting

From the assorted brown prints, cut:
- 36 squares, 3¼" × 3¼"; cut the squares into quarters diagonally to yield 144 triangles

From the assorted light prints, cut:
- 36 squares, 3¼" × 3¼"; cut the squares into quarters diagonally to yield 144 triangles

From the cream solid, cut:
- 1 square, 10" × 10"

From the taupe print, cut:
- 2 strips, 2¼" × 26¾"
- 2 strips, 2¼" × 23¼"
- 24 squares, 2¼" × 2¼"

From blue print A, cut:
- 2 strips, 2¼" × 19¾"
- 2 strips, 2¼" × 16¼"
- 4 rectangles, 2¼" × 4"

From blue print B, cut:
- 3 strips, 1½" × 42"

Making the Center Medallion

Use your favorite appliqué technique to prepare the center medallion motif using the oak leaf pattern on page 15 and the red and green prints. Center the appliqué shapes on the cream square. Pin or baste in place. Appliqué the shapes by hand or machine. Trim the completed block to 9¼" square, centering the appliqué design.

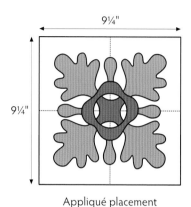

9¼"

9¼"

Appliqué placement

Making the Blocks

Press all seam allowances as indicated by the arrows.

1 Select two matching brown and two matching light triangles. Join light and dark triangles along their short edges. Sew the triangle pairs together, matching the seam intersections to make an hourglass unit. Trim the unit to measure 2¼" square, including seam allowances. Make 72 units.

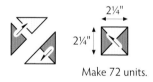

2¼"

2¼"

Make 72 units.

2 Lay out two hourglass units and two taupe squares in two rows of two. Sew the squares together into rows. Join the rows to make an Hourglass Four Patch block measuring 4" square,

including seam allowances. Make 12 blocks, paying close attention to the direction of the triangles.

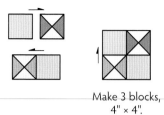

Make 3 blocks, 4" × 4".

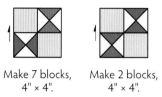

Make 7 blocks, 4" × 4".

Make 2 blocks, 4" × 4".

Making the Quilt Center

The illustrations show the orientation of the brown triangles as they appear in the quilt. Pay close attention if you want to replicate the quilt shown, or make your own quirky version!

1 Join four blocks and one blue A rectangle to make the top inner border measuring 4" × 16¼", including seam allowances. Repeat to make the bottom inner border.

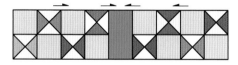

Make 1 top border, 4" × 16¼".

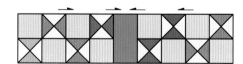

Make 1 bottom border, 4" × 16¼".

Add a dash of the **UNEXPECTED**. *Cobalt blue sashing adds extra depth to the darker hourglass unit fabrics.*

2 Join two blocks and one blue A rectangle to make the left inner border measuring 4" × 9¼", including seam allowances. Repeat to make the right inner border.

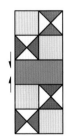 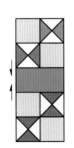

Make 1 left border,   Make 1 right border,
4" × 9¼".   4" × 9¼".

3 Sew the side inner borders to the left and right edges of the medallion center. Add the top and bottom inner borders to complete the quilt center, which should measure 16¼" square, including seam allowances.

Make 1 quilt center,
16¼" × 16¼".

Adding the Borders

1 Sew blue A 2¼" × 16¼" strips to opposite sides of the quilt center. Sew blue A 2¼" × 19¾" strips to the top and bottom of the quilt top. The quilt top should measure 19¾" square, including seam allowances.

2 Join 11 hourglass units, rotating every other unit as shown, to make the top border measuring 2¼" × 19¾", including seam allowances. Repeat to make the bottom border. Make two side borders in the same way, adding an additional hourglass unit to each end. The side borders should measure 2¼" × 23¼", including seam allowances.

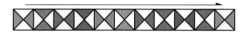

Make 2 top/bottom borders,
2¼" × 19¾".

Make 2 side borders,
2¼" × 23¼".

3 Referring to the quilt assembly diagram below, sew the 19¾"-long hourglass borders to the top and bottom of the quilt center. Sew the 23¼"-long borders to opposite sides of the quilt center. The quilt top should measure 23¼" square, including seam allowances.

4 Sew taupe 2¼" × 23¼" strips to opposite sides of the quilt top. Sew taupe 2¼" × 26¾" strips to the top and bottom of the quilt top. The quilt top should now measure 26¾" square.

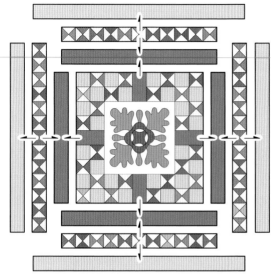

Quilt assembly

Finishing the Quilt

For detailed information about any finishing steps, visit ShopMartingale.com/HowtoQuilt.

1 Layer the quilt top, flannel or batting, and backing; baste the layers together using your preferred method.

2 Quilt by hand or machine. Timeless Traditions is machine quilted with an allover small meander design.

3 Using the blue B 1½"-wide strips, make single-fold binding (page 77) and then attach the binding to the quilt.

4 Make a label using a small piece of muslin, being sure to include your name and the date. Turn under the edges and hand stitch the label to the back of your quilt.

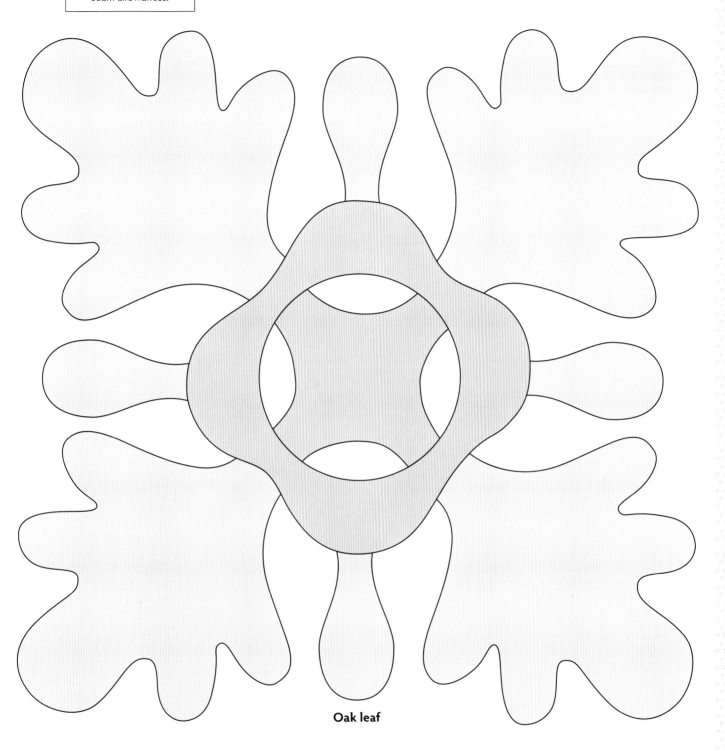

Oak leaf

Henry's Half-Square Triangles

PIECED AND HAND QUILTED BY SHERYL JOHNSON

Careful placement of humble half-square triangles gives this quilt its quirky charm. The original has all the hallmarks of a simple doll quilt created in the late 1800s. This rendition was named in honor of my second grandson, Henry, who is sweet and adorable. I'm sure you'll feel the same about Henry's Half-Square Triangles. Use contrasting colors for a visually arresting version, or for a subdued effect, choose fabrics of similar color intensity. By combining only a few favorite fabrics, you can make a unique little quilt for someone you love.

Materials

Yardage is based on 42"-wide fabric.

⅛ yard *total* of 3 assorted cream prints for blocks

⅛ yard of pink print for blocks

⅛ yard of navy print for blocks

⅛ yard of gray print for blocks

⅛ yard of rose print for blocks

⅓ yard of red print for blocks, border, and binding

½ yard of fabric for backing

15" × 23" piece of cream flannel or batting

Cutting

From each cream print, cut:
- 5 squares, 2½" × 2½" (15 total)

From the pink print, cut:
- 5 squares, 2½" × 2½"

From the navy print, cut:
- 5 squares, 2½" × 2½"

From the gray print, cut:
- 10 squares, 2½" × 2½"

From the rose print, cut:
- 10 squares, 2½" × 2½"

From the red print, cut:
- 5 squares, 2½" × 2½"
- 2 strips, 2" × 15½"
- 2 strips, 2" × 11"
- 2 strips, 1½" × 42"

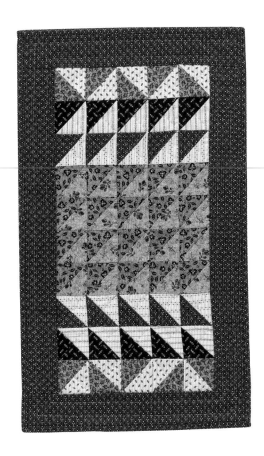

Making the Units

Press all seam allowances as indicated by the arrows.

1 Pair the 2½" squares as follows: one cream print with pink, the second cream print with navy, the third cream print with red, and gray with rose. Draw a diagonal line from corner to corner on the wrong side of the lighter square from each pair.

Stripe Savvy

When working with striped squares, be sure to mark all of them with the diagonal line and the stripe oriented in the same direction.

2 Place a marked cream square on a pink square, right sides together. Sew ¼" from both sides of the drawn line. Cut the unit apart on the marked line to make two half-square-triangle units. Trim the units to measure 2" square, including seam allowances. Make a total of 10 cream/pink units. In the same way, make 10 cream/navy, 10 cream/red, and 20 gray/rose units.

Make 10 units.

Make 10 of each unit.   Make 20 units.

Assembling the Quilt Top

1 Arrange the half-square-triangle units in 10 rows of five units each, following the color order in the quilt assembly diagram below. Pay careful attention to the orientation of the half-square triangles.

2 Sew the units together into rows. Join the rows to make the quilt center, which should measure 8" × 15½", including seam allowances.

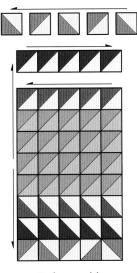

Quilt assembly

3 Sew the red 2" × 15½" strips to the sides of the quilt top. Sew the red 2" × 11" strips to the top and bottom of the quilt top. The quilt top should measure 11" × 18½".

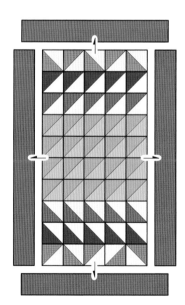

Adding the border

Finishing the Quilt

For detailed information about any finishing steps, visit ShopMartingale.com/HowtoQuilt.

1 Layer the quilt top, flannel or batting, and backing; baste the layers together using your preferred method.

2 Quilt by hand or machine. Henry's Half-Square Triangles is hand quilted in diagonal lines through the center of each block.

3 Using the red 1½"-wide strips, make single-fold binding (page 77) and then attach the binding to the quilt.

4 Make a label using a small piece of muslin, being sure to include your name and the date. Turn under the edges and hand stitch the label to the back of your quilt.

Citrus Circles

PIECED AND HAND QUILTED BY SHERYL JOHNSON

The fun, spirited color palette in this quilt is reminiscent of the circa-1870 quilt that inspired it. Look closely and you'll discover that each of the appliquéd citrus-peel shapes is made from a 1" patchwork block surrounded by its own little Crazy quilt! A log cabin–style border contains little surprises here and there. Gather all your favorite bits and pieces, and sink your teeth into this juicy project.

Materials

Yardage is based on 42"-wide fabric.

1⅝ yards *total* of assorted light, medium, and dark prints in greens, blues, creams, cheddars, browns, reds, blacks, and pinks for blocks, crazy piecing, borders, and binding

⅝ yard of gray print for background

¾ yard of fabric for backing

27" × 27" piece of cream flannel or batting

Air-soluble marking pen

Freezer paper (optional)

Making the Blocks

The block instructions are for one of each design; repeat to make the number of blocks indicated. Press all seam allowances as indicated by the arrows.

BOW TIE

Make one Bow Tie block as follows. Repeat to make five blocks.

From a dark print, cut:
- 2 squares, ¾" × ¾"
- 2 squares, 1" × 1"

From a light print, cut:
- 2 squares, 1" × 1"

1 Draw a diagonal line from corner to corner on the wrong side of the dark ¾" squares. Place a marked square on one corner of a light square. Sew on the marked line. If desired, trim the excess corner fabric ¼" from the stitched line. Make two units measuring 1" square, including seam allowances.

Make 2 units,
1" × 1".

21

Lay out the 1" squares in two rows of two. Sew the squares together into rows. Join the rows to make a Four Patch block measuring 1½" square, including seam allowances. Make a total of six blocks.

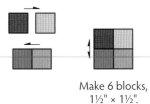

Make 6 blocks,
1½" × 1½".

PINWHEEL

Make one Pinwheel block as follows. Repeat to make five blocks.

From a dark print, cut:

- 2 squares, 1½" × 1½"

From a light print, cut:

- 2 squares, 1½" × 1½"

1 Draw a diagonal line from corner to corner on the wrong side of the light 1½" squares. Layer a marked square and a dark square right sides together. Sew ¼" from both sides of the line. Cut the unit apart on the marked line to make two half-square-triangle units. Trim the units to measure 1" square, including seam allowances.

Make 4 units.

2 Arrange the half-square-triangle units in two rows of two, noting the orientation of each unit. Sew the units together into rows. Join the rows to make a Pinwheel block measuring 1½" square, including seam allowances. Make five blocks.

Make 5 blocks,
1½" × 1½".

2 Lay out the units and dark 1" squares in two rows of two, noting the orientation of the units. Sew the squares and units together into rows. Join the rows to make a Bow Tie block measuring 1½" square, including seam allowances. Make a total of five blocks.

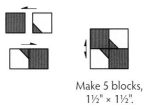

Make 5 blocks,
1½" × 1½".

FOUR PATCH

Make one Four Patch block as follows. Repeat to make six blocks.

From the assorted light, medium, and dark prints, cut:

- 4 squares, 1" × 1"

HALF-SQUARE TRIANGLE

Make two Half-Square Triangle blocks as follows. Repeat to make 10 blocks. You'll use one block of each color combination. The five leftover blocks can be saved for a future quirky project.

From a dark print, cut:

- 1 square, 2" × 2"

From a light or medium print, cut:

- 1 square, 2" × 2"

Make one Half-Square Triangle block as described in step 1 of the Pinwheel block on page 22. Trim the block to measure 1½" square, including seam allowances.

Make 10 blocks.

BROKEN DISHES

Make one Broken Dishes block as follows. Repeat to make five blocks.

From a dark print, cut:

- 2 squares, 1½" × 1½"

From a light print, cut:

- 2 squares, 1½" × 1½"

1 Make four half-square-triangle units as described in step 1 of the Pinwheel block on page 22. Trim the units to measure 1" square, including seam allowances.

2 Arrange the half-square-triangle units in two rows of two, noting the orientation of each unit. Sew the units together into rows. Join the rows to make a Broken Dishes block measuring 1½" square, including seam allowances. Make five blocks.

Make 5 blocks,
1½" × 1½".

BIRDS IN THE AIR

Make one Birds in the Air block as follows. Repeat to make five blocks.

From a dark print, cut:

- 1 square, 1½" × 1½"

From a medium print, cut:

- 1 square, 1" × 1"

From a light print, cut:

- 1 square, 1½" × 1½"
- 1 square, 1" × 1"

1 Make two half-square-triangle units as described in step 1 of the Pinwheel block on page 22. Trim the units to measure 1" square, including the seam allowances.

2 Arrange the half-square-triangle units, medium square, and light 1" square in two rows of two, noting the orientation of each unit. Sew the units together into rows. Join the rows to make a Birds in the Air block measuring 1½" square, including seam allowances. Make a total of five blocks.

Make 5 blocks,
1½" × 1½".

TRIANGLE FOUR PATCH

Make one Triangle Four Patch block as follows. Repeat to make five blocks.

From a dark print or assorted dark prints, cut:

- 2 squares, 1½" × 1½"

From a light print or assorted light prints, cut:

- 2 squares, 1½" × 1½"

1 Make four half-square-triangle units as described in step 1 of the Pinwheel block on page 22. Trim the units to measure 1" square, including the seam allowances.

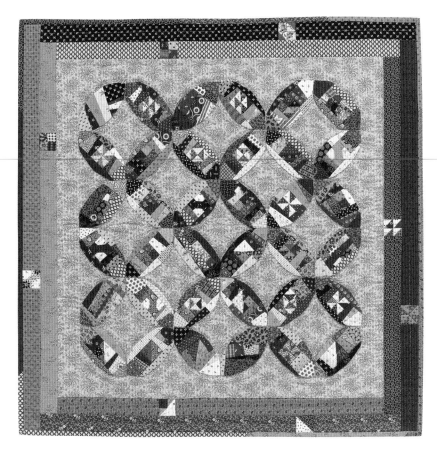

Tiny traditional blocks are hidden inside **CRAZY QUILT PATCHES** *that have been cut into orange-peel shapes to form the quilt center.*

2 Arrange the units in two rows of two, noting the orientation of each unit. Sew the units together into rows. Join the rows to make a Triangle Four Patch block measuring 1½" square, including seam allowances. Make a total of five blocks.

Make 5 blocks,
1½" × 1½".

Finishing the Blocks

Now that the blocks are made, it's time to add the crazy part. Set aside two Four Patch blocks and one of each of the Pinwheel, Broken Dishes, Bow Tie, Half-Square Triangle, Birds in the Air, and Four Patch Triangle blocks for the borders.

1 Cut a variety of strips in differing widths from the light, medium, and dark prints.

2 Sew strips to opposite sides of a block. Trim the strips even with the edges of the block, and then trim them at a "crazy" angle. Continue adding strips and trimming them until the piece measures at least 1½" × 4¼". Make 28 strips.

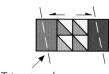 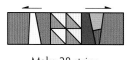

Trim at angle.   Make 28 strips,
1½" × 4¼".

3 Sew strips at least 1" wide to the top and bottom of a crazy-pieced unit. Make 28 units measuring 3" × 4¼".

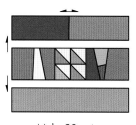

Make 28 units,
3" × 4¼".

4 In the same way, sew together scraps and strips to make a crazy-pieced unit measuring at least 3" × 4¼". Make eight crazy-pieced units.

Making the Quilt Center

From the gray print, cut:

- 1 square, 19" × 19"

1 Using an air-soluble marking pen, draw a vertical line and a horizontal line to mark the center of the gray square. Measure 2¾" from the vertical center line and draw a line on each side of the center line. Draw a total of three lines, 2¾" apart, on each side of the vertical line. In the same way, draw horizontal lines to make a grid.

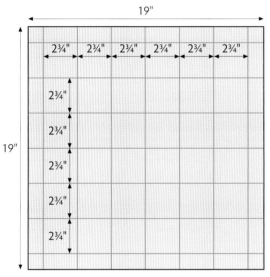

Mark lines.

2 Using your favorite appliqué technique and the citrus-peel pattern on page 27, prepare the crazy-pieced units for appliqué. This project does not lend itself to fusible appliqué; I used freezer paper to prepare the citrus peels, adding a seam allowance outside of the freezer-paper shape.

3 Referring to the photo on page 24 and the quilt assembly diagram on page 26, position the prepared citrus peels on the gray square, placing them diagonally in the grid squares and making sure the ends are touching where the grid lines intersect. Appliqué the citrus peels by hand or machine.

Adding the Borders

From a green print, cut:

- 1 strip, 1½" × 6"
- 1 strip, 1½" × 12½"
- 1 strip, 1½" × 21", for binding

From a blue print, cut:

- 1 strip, 1½" × 9"
- 1 strip, 1½" × 10½"
- 1 strip, 1½" × 18", for binding

From a light print, cut:

- 1 strip, 1½" × 6½"
- 1 strip, 1½" × 13"
- 1 strip, 1½" × 18", for binding

From a cheddar print, cut:

- 1 strip, 1½" × 5½"
- 1 strip, 1½" × 15"
- 1 strip, 1½" × 13", for binding

From a brown print, cut:

- 1 strip, 1½" × 5½"
- 1 strip, 1½" × 15"
- 1 strip, 1½" × 13", for binding

From a red print, cut:

- 1 strip, 1½" × 6½"
- 1 strip, 1½" × 15"
- 1 strip, 1½" × 18", for binding

From a black print, cut:

- 1 strip, 1½" × 7½"
- 1 strip, 1½" × 14"

From a pink print, cut:

- 1 strip, 1½" × 8½"
- 1 strip, 1½" × 14"
- 1 strip, 1½" × 13", for binding

1 Referring to the quilt photo and the quilt
  assembly diagram, sew each of the remaining
1½" blocks between two matching strips to make the
following borders, pressing seam allowances away
from the block:

- Green border measuring 1½" × 19", including
  seam allowances.

- Blue border measuring 1½" × 20", including
  seam allowances.

- Light border measuring 1½" × 20", including
  seam allowances.

- Cheddar border measuring 1½" × 21", including
  seam allowances.

- Brown border measuring 1½" × 21", including
  seam allowances.

- Red border measuring 1½" × 22", including
  seam allowances.

- Black border measuring 1½" × 22", including
  seam allowances.

- Pink border measuring 1½" × 23", including
  seam allowances.

2 Sew the green border to the bottom of the quilt
  center. Working in a counterclockwise direction,
add the blue border, the light border, and then the
cheddar border. The quilt top should measure 21"
square, including seam allowances.

3 Sew the brown border to the bottom of the
  quilt top. Add the red border, the black border,
and then the pink border in a counterclockwise
direction. The quilt top should measure 23" square.

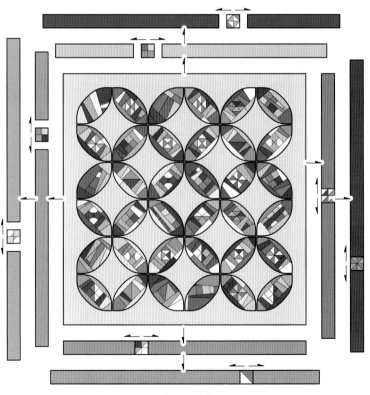

Quilt assembly

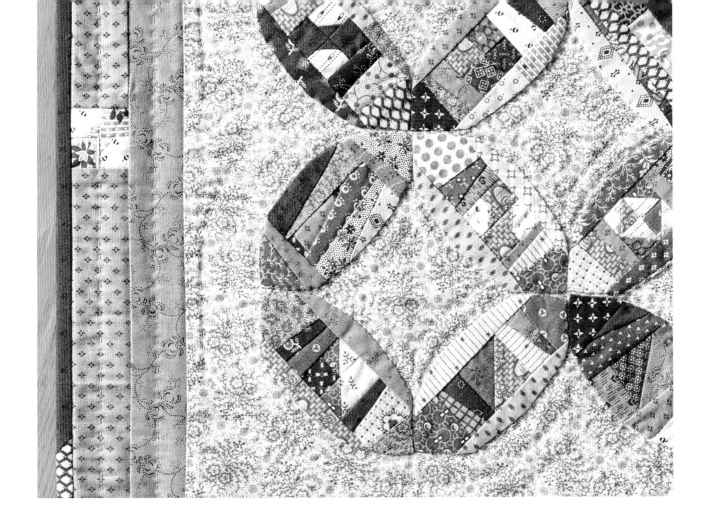

Finishing the Quilt

For detailed information about any finishing steps, visit ShopMartingale.com/HowtoQuilt.

1 Layer the quilt top, flannel or batting, and backing; baste the layers together using your preferred method.

2 Quilt by hand or machine. Citrus Circles is hand quilted, with an echo pattern outlining each citrus peel.

3 Using a variety of 1½"-wide print strips, make scrappy single-fold binding (page 77) and then attach the binding to the quilt.

4 Make a label using a small piece of muslin, being sure to include your name and the date. Turn under the edges and hand stitch the label to the back of your quilt.

Pattern does not include seam allowances.

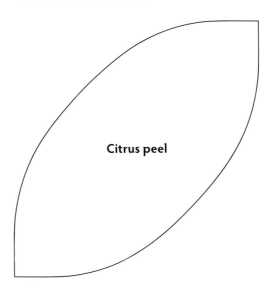

Citrus peel

Lemon LeMoyne

PIECED BY SHERYL JOHNSON AND MACHINE QUILTED BY DEBBIE BLAIR

A bright lemon-yellow print is an unexpected setting for these antique LeMoyne stars, which were probably named for the French sculptor who created star-patterned tiles for the Versailles palace in the early 18th century. Just a few different prints, careful fabric placement, and a modern construction technique make these blocks go together quickly and easily. Search your scraps for soft vintage fabrics with a worn-over-time appeal, and you'll be on your way to creating today's version of a lovely antique heirloom.

Materials

Yardage is based on 42"-wide fabric.

⅛ yard *each* of 3 assorted cream prints (A, B, and C) for blocks

⅛ yard *each* of pink, gray, rose, and brown prints for blocks

¼ yard *total* of 2 different black prints for blocks

¼ yard of ivory solid for blocks

⅛ yard of tan print for sashing

⅜ yard of yellow print for sashing, border, and binding

⅝ yard of fabric for backing

22" × 32" piece of cream flannel or batting

Cutting

From cream print A, cut:
- 16 squares, 2" × 2"
- 16 squares, 1½" × 1½"

From cream print B, cut:
- 20 squares, 2" × 2"
- 20 squares, 1½" × 1½"

From cream print C, cut:
- 24 squares, 2" × 2"
- 24 squares, 1½" × 1½"

From each of the pink and gray prints, cut:
- 16 squares, 2" × 2" (32 total)

Continued on page 30

29

Continued from page 29

From each of the rose and brown prints, cut:

- 20 squares, 2" × 2" (40 total)

From the black prints, cut a total of:

- 24 squares, 2" × 2"

From the ivory solid, cut:

- 24 squares, 2" × 2"

From the tan print, cut:

- 12 rectangles, 1½" × 4½"

From the yellow print, cut:

- 2 strips, 2" × 27½"
- 2 strips, 2" × 14½"
- 3 strips, 1½" × 42"
- 2 strips, 1½" × 24½"

Making the Blocks

Press all seam allowances as indicated by the arrows.

1 Pair the following 2" squares; for each pair of squares, draw a diagonal line from corner to corner on the wrong side of the lighter square:

- 8 pink and 8 gray squares

- 8 pink and 8 cream A squares

- 8 gray and 8 cream A squares

- 10 rose and 10 brown squares

- 10 rose and 10 cream B squares

- 10 brown and 10 cream B squares

- 12 black and 12 ivory squares

- 12 black and 12 cream C squares

- 12 ivory and 12 cream C squares

LeMoyne Stars with a worn-over-time appeal are **HIGHLIGHTED** *with a pop of lemon yellow.*

2 Starting with the pink and gray squares, layer the marked square on the unmarked square, right sides together. Sew ¼" from both sides of the drawn line. Cut on the line to yield two half-square-triangle units. Trim the units to measure 1½" square, including seam allowances. Repeat to make the required number of units from each color combination.

Make 16 units.

Make 16 of each unit.

Make 20 of each unit.

Make 24 of each unit.

3 Arrange four pink/gray units, four pink/cream units, four gray/cream units, and four matching cream 1½" squares in four rows, noting the orientation of the half-square-triangle units. The cream squares should match the cream used in the half-square-triangle units. Sew the units and squares together in rows. Join the rows to make a block measuring 4½" square, including seam

allowances. Repeat to make four pink/gray blocks, five rose/brown blocks, and six black/ivory blocks.

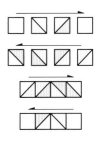

Make 4 blocks,
4½" × 4½".

Make 4 blocks,
4½" × 4½".

Make 1 block,
4½" × 4½".

Make 6 blocks,
4½" × 4½".

Assembling the Quilt Top

1 Refer to the photo on page 30 and the assembly diagram on page 32 for placement guidance. Lay out five blocks and four tan 1½" × 4½" rectangles, beginning and ending with a block. Join the blocks and rectangles to make a column measuring 4½" × 24½", including seam allowances. Make three columns.

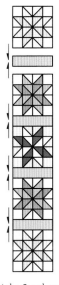

Make 3 columns,
4½" × 24½".

2 Join the columns and yellow 1½" × 24½" strips, taking care to align the tan sashing strips horizontally. The quilt center should measure 14½" × 24½", including seam allowances.

3 Sew the yellow 2" × 14½" strips to the top and bottom of the quilt top. Sew the yellow 2" × 27½" strips to the sides of the quilt top. The quilt top should measure 17½" × 27½".

Finishing the Quilt

For detailed information about any finishing steps, visit ShopMartingale.com/HowtoQuilt.

1 Layer the quilt top, flannel or batting, and backing; baste the layers together using your preferred method.

2 Quilt by hand or machine. Lemon LeMoyne is machine quilted in an allover small meander design.

3 Using the yellow 1½" × 42" strips, make single-fold binding (page 77) and then attach the binding to the quilt.

4 Make a label using a small piece of muslin, being sure to include your name and the date. Turn under the edges and hand stitch the label to the back of your quilt.

Quilt assembly

Kenny's Courthouse

PIECED BY SHERYL JOHNSON AND MACHINE QUILTED BY DEBBIE BLAIR

The hourglass in the center of these Courthouse Steps blocks gives Kenny's Courthouse a bold geometric twist. Here the quirkiness comes from the unique placement of color, which makes the block-building process a whole lot of fun. Kenny, my first grandson, loves his Legos and can spend hours making sure things look just right. If you aren't afraid to let color speak loudly, then this is sure to become one of your favorite block-building projects.

Materials

Yardage is based on 42"-wide fabric.

¼ yard of tan print for blocks

¼ yard of cream print for blocks

¼ yard of red print for blocks

⅓ yard of green print for blocks

¼ yard of navy print for blocks

¾ yard of pink print for blocks, middle border, and binding

⅞ yard of yellow print for blocks and borders

1¼ yards of fabric for backing

31" × 41" piece of cream flannel or batting

Attention to detail and **BOLD COLOR** *combine in this unexpected quilt.*

Cutting

From the tan print, cut:
- 2 squares, 2½" × 2½"; cut the squares into quarters diagonally to yield 8 triangles (3 are extra)
- 3 strips, 1" × 42"

From the cream print, cut:
- 2 squares, 2½" × 2½"; cut the squares into quarters diagonally to yield 8 triangles
- 4 strips, 1" × 42"

From the red print, cut:
- 2 squares, 2½" × 2½"; cut the squares into quarters diagonally to yield 8 triangles
- 4 strips, 1" × 42"

From the green print, cut:
- 4 squares, 2½" × 2½"; cut the squares into quarters diagonally to yield 16 triangles (2 are extra)
- 6 strips, 1" × 42"

From the navy print, cut:
- 3 squares, 2½" × 2½"; cut the squares into quarters diagonally to yield 12 triangles (2 are extra)
- 5 strips, 1" × 42"

From the pink print, cut:
- 7 squares, 2½" × 2½"; cut the squares into quarters diagonally to yield 28 triangles (2 are extra)
- 4 strips, 1½" × 42"
- 2 strips, 1½" × 34½"
- 2 strips, 1½" × 22½"
- 10 strips, 1" × 42"

From the yellow print, cut:
- 7 squares, 2½" × 2½"; cut the squares into quarters diagonally to yield 28 triangles (3 are extra)
- 2 strips, 1½" × 36½"
- 2 strips, 1½" × 32½"
- 2 strips, 1½" × 24½"
- 2 strips, 1½" × 20½"
- 11 strips, 1" × 42"

Making the Blocks

Building Courthouse Steps blocks in an assembly line is simpler than cutting the 1"-wide strips into the required lengths. Follow the steps below and all 24 blocks will be completed before you know it. Press all seam allowances in the direction indicated by the arrows.

1 Working on a flat surface and referring to the hourglass layout diagram, arrange 96 triangles to form 24 squares.

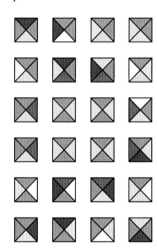

Hourglass layout

2 Using one set of triangles, join the triangles along their short edges. Sew the triangle pairs together, matching the seam intersections to make an hourglass unit. Trim the unit to measure 1½" square, including seam allowances. Make 24 units. Referring to the hourglass layout on page 35, insert a small pin to mark the top of each block.

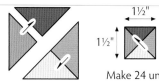

Make 24 units.

3 Separate the hourglass units into piles, grouping them by the color at the top of the unit.

4 With right sides together, chain piece the top of an hourglass unit to the matching 1"-wide strip. Continue stitching all the units of a particular color. Roughly trim the 1"-wide strip and then chain piece the next color. Repeat until all the units are stitched to a coordinating 1"-wide strip. Remove the chain from your sewing machine and cut the units apart. You should have 24 units.

5 Repeat steps 3 and 4 to chain piece the bottom of each unit to a matching 1" strip. Make 24 units. Trim the units to measure 1½" × 2½", including seam allowances.

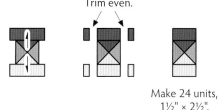

Make 24 units,
1½" × 2½".

6 Chain piece matching 1"-wide strips to each side of the unit. Make 24 units and trim them to 2½" square, including seam allowances.

Make 24 units,
2½" × 2½".

7 Continue as before, chain piecing matching strips to each edge of the center unit. After adding strips to opposite sides of the unit, trim the unit to the measurements listed below. Make 24 blocks measuring 5½" square, including seam allowances.

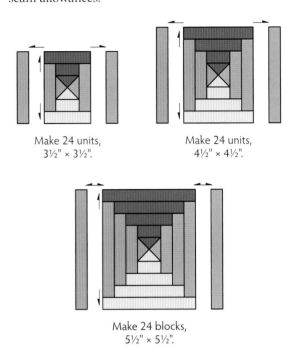

Make 24 units,
3½" × 3½".

Make 24 units,
4½" × 4½".

Make 24 blocks,
5½" × 5½".

Assembling the Quilt Top

1 Referring to the quilt assembly diagram at right, lay out the blocks, paying careful attention to the orientation of each block. Sew the blocks together into rows. Join the rows, matching seam intersections. The quilt top should measure 20½" × 30½", including seam allowances.

2 Sew the yellow 1½" × 20½" strips to the top and bottom of the quilt top. Sew the yellow 1½" × 32½" strips to the sides of the quilt top. The quilt top should measure 22½" × 32½", including seam allowances.

3 Sew the pink 1½" × 22½" strips to the top and bottom of the quilt top. Sew the pink 1½" × 34½" strips to the sides of the quilt top. The quilt top should measure 24½" × 34½", including seam allowances.

4 Sew the yellow 1½" × 24½" strips to the top and bottom of the quilt top. Sew the yellow 1½" × 36½" strips to the sides of the quilt top. The quilt top should measure 26½" × 36½".

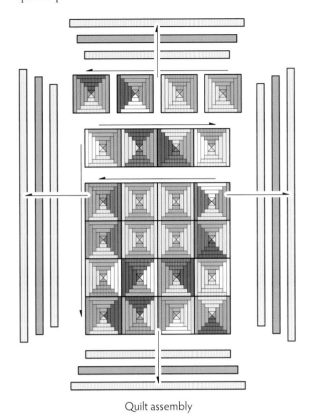

Quilt assembly

Finishing the Quilt

For detailed information about any finishing steps, visit ShopMartingale.com/HowtoQuilt.

1 Layer the quilt top, flannel or batting, and backing; baste the layers together.

2 Quilt by hand or machine. Kenny's Courthouse is machine quilted with an allover small meander design.

3 Using the pink 1½" × 42" strips, make single-fold binding (page 77) and then attach the binding to the quilt.

4 Make a label using a small piece of muslin, being sure to include your name and the date. Turn under the edges and hand stitch the label to the back of your quilt.

Nine Patch Posy

PIECED AND HAND QUILTED BY SHERYL JOHNSON

The hardworking Nine Patch, the most common of blocks, sets the stage *for a perfectly graphic posy blooming in the center. Reach into your scrap basket for a variety of reds, browns, grays, and blacks to create a faultless color combination for this circa-1880 doll quilt. The geometric simplicity of the Nine Patch blocks is a fitting counterpoint to the center flower medallion. A little hand quilting is all you need to give this project the finishing flourish.*

Materials

Yardage is based on 42"-wide fabric.

¼ yard *total* of assorted medium to dark prints in reds, browns, grays, and blacks for blocks

⅝ yard of cream solid for blocks

1 square, 6" × 6", of red print for flower medallion appliqué

1 square, 4" × 4", of brown print for flower medallion appliqué

¼ yard of black print for binding

⅝ yard of fabric for backing

21" × 25" piece of cream flannel or batting

Cutting

From assorted medium to dark prints, cut:

- 28 sets of 5 matching squares, 1¼" × 1¼" (140 total)

From the cream solid, cut:

- 1 square, 7¼" × 7¼"

- 2 strips, 2¾" × 42"; crosscut into 26 squares, 2¾" × 2¾"

- 4 strips, 1¼" × 42"; crosscut into 112 squares, 1¼" × 1¼"

From the black print, cut:

- 3 strips, 1½" × 42"

*The simple Nine Patch block is the perfect partner, letting the **POSY MEDALLION** be the center of attention.*

Making the Center Block

Using your favorite appliqué technique, prepare the appliqué motif using the red 6" square, brown 4" square, and the patterns on page 41. Position the appliqué shapes in the center of the cream 7¼" square. Pin or baste in place. Appliqué the shapes by hand or machine.

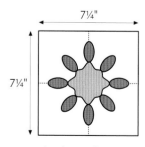

Appliqué placement

Making the Nine Patch Blocks

Press all seam allowances as indicated by the arrows.

Lay out five matching medium or dark 1¼" squares and four cream 1¼" squares in three rows of three. Sew the squares together to make a Nine Patch block measuring 2¾" square, including seam allowances. Make 28 blocks.

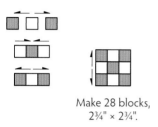

Make 28 blocks,
2¾" × 2¾".

Assembling the Quilt Top

1 Arrange 11 Nine Patch blocks and 10 cream 2¾" squares in three horizontal rows, alternating the blocks and squares in each row and from row to row. Sew the blocks together into rows. Join the rows to make the top section, measuring 7¼" × 16¼", including seam allowances. Repeat to make the bottom section.

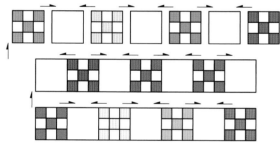

Make 2 top/bottom sections,
7¼" × 16¼".

2 Lay out three rows of one block and one square each. Sew the blocks and squares together into rows. Join the rows to make a side section measuring 5" × 7¼", including seam allowances. Repeat to make a second side section.

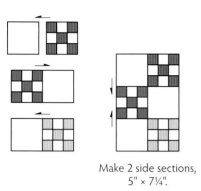

Make 2 side sections,
5" × 7¼".

3 Join the side sections to the appliquéd center block to make the center section. Sew the top and bottom sections to the center section to complete the quilt top, which should measure 16¼" × 20¾".

Quilt assembly

Finishing the Quilt

For detailed information about any finishing steps, visit ShopMartingale.com/HowtoQuilt.

1 Layer the quilt top, flannel or batting, and backing; baste the layers together using your preferred method.

2 Quilt by hand or machine. Nine Patch Posy is hand quilted in a diagonal crosshatch pattern through the center of each block. The center medallion is echo quilted around the posy.

3 Using the black 1½"-wide strips, make single-fold binding (page 77) and then attach the binding to the quilt.

4 Make a label using a small piece of muslin, being sure to include your name and the date. Turn under the edges and hand stitch the label to the back of your quilt.

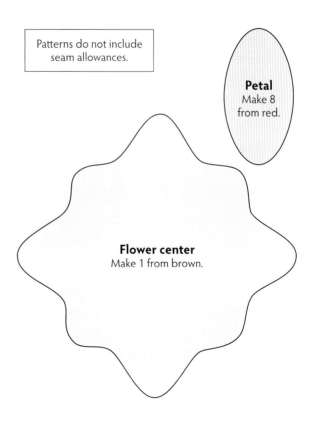

Patterns do not include seam allowances.

Petal
Make 8
from red.

Flower center
Make 1 from brown.

Rickrack Rows

PIECED BY SHERYL JOHNSON AND MACHINE QUILTED BY DEBBIE BLAIR

Uniform rows of Square-in-a-Square blocks create a pattern reminiscent of rickrack, a braided zigzag trim that was ubiquitous in the 1950s and '60s. The inspiration for this reproduction quilt was a mid-nineteenth-century gem with the soft vintage feel of a well-loved favorite. Pay close attention to contrasting color placement so that your cherished fabric pieces will pull off the overall light feeling of this scrappy sensation. Surely this new treasure will become someone else's adored favorite too.

Materials

Yardage is based on 42"-wide fabric.

1¼ yards *total* of assorted medium and dark prints for blocks (collectively referred to as "dark")

½ yard *total* of assorted light prints for blocks

1½ yards of cream print for setting triangles and sashing

¼ yard of blue print for binding

1⅜ yards of fabric for backing

39" × 49" piece of cream flannel or batting

Cutting

From the assorted dark prints, cut:

- 86 pairs of matching squares, 2½" × 2½"; cut the squares in half diagonally to yield 4 matching triangles (344 total)

- 86 squares, 1¾" × 1¾"

From the assorted light prints, cut:

- 86 squares, 2½" × 2½"; cut each square into quarters diagonally to yield 4 matching triangles (344 total)

From the cream print, cut:

- 5 strips, 5" × 42"; crosscut into 32 squares, 5" × 5". Cut the squares into quarters diagonally to yield 128 side triangles.

- 2 strips, 3½" × 42"; crosscut into 16 squares, 3½" × 3½". Cut the squares in half diagonally to yield 32 corner triangles.

- 1 strip, 3" × 42"; crosscut into 12 squares, 3" × 3"

- 9 strips, 1½" × 33"

From the blue print, cut:

- 5 strips, 1½" × 42"

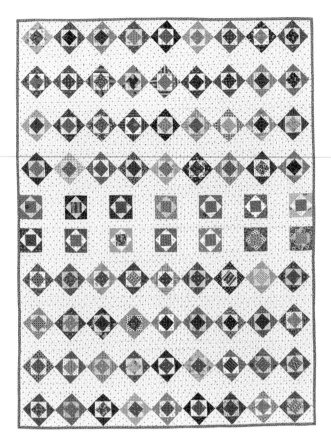

Have you ever seen a quilt like this where the blocks are all **SET ON POINT**—*except for those in two of the rows?*

Making the Blocks

Press all seam allowances as indicated by the arrows.

1 Fold a dark square in half vertically and horizontally, and lightly crease to mark the center of each side. Fold four matching light triangles in half, and lightly crease to mark the center of the long side. Stitch triangles to opposite sides of the square, matching the center creases. Stitch triangles to the remaining sides of the square. The unit should measure 2¼" square, including seam allowances. Make 86 units.

Make 86 units,
2¼" × 2¼".

2 Fold four matching dark triangles in half, and lightly crease to mark the center of the long side. Stitch triangles to opposite sides of the unit, matching the center creases to the crossed seams. Stitch triangles to the remaining sides of the unit to make a Square-in-a-Square block. Trim the block to measure 3" square, including the seam allowances. Make 86 blocks.

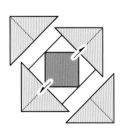 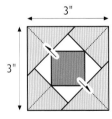

Make 86 blocks.

Assembling the Quilt Top

1 Arrange nine blocks, 16 cream side triangles, and four cream corner triangles in diagonal rows. Sew the side triangles and blocks together to make diagonal rows. Join the diagonal rows, matching the seam intersections. Add the corner triangles last. Trim and square up the row to measure 4" × 33", including seam allowances. Along the top and bottom edges, make sure to leave ¼" beyond the points of the blocks for seam allowances. Make eight rows.

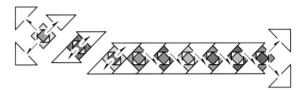

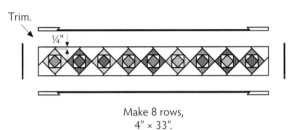

Make 8 rows,
4" × 33".

2 Join seven blocks and six cream 3" squares to make a row measuring 3" × 33", including seam allowances. Repeat to make a second row.

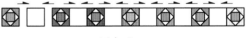

Make 2 rows,
3" × 33".

3 Lay out the rows and cream 1½" × 33" strips, alternating them as shown in the quilt assembly diagram at right. Join the rows to complete the quilt top, which should measure 33" × 42½".

Finishing the Quilt

For detailed information about any finishing steps, visit ShopMartingale.com/HowtoQuilt.

1 Layer the quilt top, flannel or batting, and backing; baste the layers together using your preferred method.

2 Quilt by hand or machine. Rickrack Rows is machine quilted in an allover small meander design.

3 Using the blue 1½"-wide strips, make single-fold binding (page 77) and then attach the binding to the quilt.

4 Make a label using a small piece of muslin, being sure to include your name and the date. Turn under the edges and hand stitch the label to the back of your quilt.

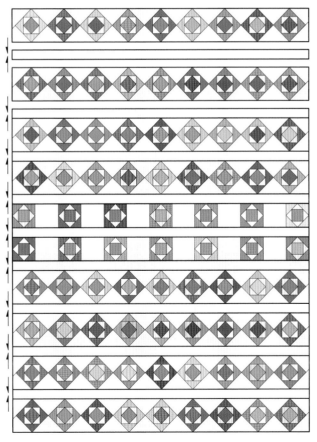

Quilt assembly

Building Blocks

PIECED BY SHERYL JOHNSON AND MACHINE QUILTED BY DEBBIE BLAIR

Put your sewing basket to the test as you search for the perfect scraps to fabricate the blocks in this structural sampler. Pinwheel, Evening Star, Four Patch, and Basket blocks all combine to create a construction project that's sure to put a smile on your face. Once you manufacture a pile of these simple classic blocks, you're ready to set the blocks in simple rows, stand back, and enjoy your new one-of-a-kind sampler, Building Blocks.

Materials

Yardage is based on 42"-wide fabric.

⅞ yard *total* of assorted light, medium, and dark prints for blocks

¼ yard of ivory solid for blocks

⅛ yard of red solid for blocks

⅛ yard of blue print for blocks

¼ yard of brown print for binding

¾ yard of fabric for backing

25" × 29" piece of cream flannel or batting

Cutting for Filler Blocks and Binding

Refer to the quilt photo on page 49 and the assembly diagram on page 52 for fabric and color inspiration. Cutting information for the seven block designs is included with each set of block instructions.

From the light, medium, and dark prints, cut a total of:
- 8 rectangles, 2½" × 4½"

From the brown print, cut:
- 3 strips, 1½" × 42"

Making the Blocks

The block instructions are for one of each design; repeat to make the number of blocks indicated. Press all seam allowances in the direction indicated by the arrows.

STAR

Make one Star block as follows. Repeat to make four blocks, reversing the light and dark prints for two of the blocks.

From a medium or dark print, cut:

- 1 square, 3¼" × 3¼"; cut the square into quarters diagonally to yield 4 triangles
- 4 squares, 1½" × 1½"

From the ivory solid or a light print, cut:

- 1 square, 2½" × 2½"
- 4 squares, 1⅞" × 1⅞"; cut the squares in half diagonally to yield 8 triangles

1 Sew an ivory triangle to the short side of a medium or dark triangle; press. Sew an ivory triangle to the other short side of the medium or dark triangle to make a flying-geese unit. The unit should measure 1½" × 2½", including seam allowances. Make a total of four units.

Make 4 units,
1½" × 2½".

2 Arrange the flying-geese units, ivory 2½" square, and medium or dark 1½" squares in three rows. Sew the units and squares together into rows. Join the rows to make a Star block measuring 4½" square, including seam allowances. Make four blocks.

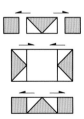

Make 4 blocks,
4½" × 4½".

FOUR PATCH

Make one Four Patch block as follows. Repeat to make seven blocks.

From the assorted light, medium, and dark prints, cut:

- 2 pairs of matching squares, 2½" × 2½"

Lay out the 2½" squares in two rows of two. Sew the squares together into rows. Join the rows to make a Four Patch block measuring 4½" square, including seam allowances. Make a total of seven blocks.

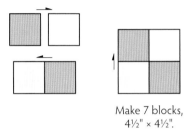

Make 7 blocks,
4½" × 4½".

BASKET

Make one Basket block as follows. Repeat to make four blocks.

From a dark print, cut:

- 1 square, 2⅞" × 2⅞"; cut the square in half diagonally to yield 2 triangles (1 is extra)
- 3 squares, 2" × 2"
- 1 square, 1⅞" × 1⅞"; cut the square in half diagonally to yield 2 triangles

From a light print, cut:

- 1 square, 2⅞" × 2⅞"; cut the square in half diagonally to yield 2 triangles (1 is extra)
- 3 squares, 2" × 2"
- 1 square, 1⅞" × 1⅞"; cut the square in half diagonally to yield 2 triangles
- 2 rectangles, 1½" × 2½"

*Scrap basket samplers are a great opportunity for testing **UNIQUE** block and color combinations that you wouldn't usually put together.*

1 Draw a diagonal line from corner to corner on the wrong side of the light 2" squares. Layer a marked square on top of a dark 2" square, right sides together. Sew ¼" from both sides of the drawn line. Cut on the line to yield two half-square-triangle units. Trim the units to measure 1½" square, including seam allowances. Make six units.

Make 6 units.

2 Sew one short edge of a dark 1⅞" triangle to a short edge of a light 1½" × 2½" rectangle, making sure the other short edge of the triangle is flush with the long side of the rectangle as shown. Make a second mirror-image unit.

Make 1 of each unit.

3 Arrange the half-square-triangle units and light 1⅞" triangles in three rows. Join the units and light triangles into rows. Join the rows and add the dark 2⅞" triangle to the bottom of unit to make the basket body. The unit should measure 3½" square, including seam allowances.

Make 1 unit, 3½" × 3½".

4 Sew the mirror-image units from step 2 to the basket-body unit. Add the light 2⅞" triangle to complete the Basket block. The block should measure 4½" square, including seam allowances. Make a total of four blocks.

Make 4 blocks,
4½" × 4½".

SMALL PINWHEEL

Make 16 Small Pinwheel blocks as follows.

From the red solid, cut:

- 16 squares, 2" × 2"

From the blue print, cut:

- 16 squares, 2" × 2"

From the ivory solid, cut:

- 32 squares, 2" × 2"

1 Use the red squares and 16 ivory squares to make 32 half-square-triangle units as described in step 1 of "Basket" on page 49. Trim each unit to measure 1½" square, including seam allowances. Repeat to make 32 units using the blue squares and the remaining ivory squares.

2 Arrange four matching half-square-triangle units in two rows of two, noting the orientation of each unit. Sew the units together into rows. Join the rows to make a Pinwheel block measuring 2½" square, including seam allowances. Make eight red and eight blue Pinwheel blocks.

Make 8 of each block,
2½" × 2½".

3 Join two matching blocks to make a double Pinwheel block measuring 2½" × 4½", including seam allowances. Make two red and two blue blocks. The remaining small Pinwheel blocks will be used to make Pinwheel Four Patch blocks.

Make 2 of each block,
2½" × 4½".

PINWHEEL FOUR PATCH

Make one Pinwheel Four Patch block as follows. Repeat to make four blocks.

From a light, medium, or dark print, cut:

- 2 squares, 2½" × 2½"

Lay out two matching Small Pinwheel blocks and two matching print 2½" squares. Sew the blocks and squares together into rows. Join the rows to make a Pinwheel Four Patch block measuring 4½" square, including seam allowances. Make a total of four blocks.

Make 4 blocks,
4½" × 4½".

LARGE PINWHEEL

Make one Large Pinwheel block as follows. Repeat to make three blocks.

From a dark print, cut:

- 2 squares, 3" × 3"

From a light print, cut:

- 2 squares, 3" × 3"

1 Use the light and dark squares to make four half-square-triangle units as described in step 1 of "Basket" on page 49. Trim each unit to measure 2½" square, including seam allowances.

2 Arrange the half-square-triangle units in two rows of two, noting the orientation of each unit. Sew the units together into rows. Join the rows to make a Pinwheel block measuring 4½" square, including seam allowances. Make two blocks that are mirror images.

Make 1 block,
4½" × 4½".

Make 2 blocks,
4½" × 4½".

NINE PATCH VARIATION

Make one Nine Patch Variation block as follows. Repeat to make two blocks.

From a dark print, cut:

- 1 square, 1⅞" × 1⅞"
- 4 rectangles, 1½" × 2½"

From a light print, cut:

- 2 squares, 2" × 2"; cut the squares in half diagonally to yield 4 triangles
- 4 squares, 1½" × 1½"

1 Fold the dark square in half vertically and horizontally, and lightly crease to mark the center of each side. Fold the light triangles in half, and lightly crease to mark the center of the long side. Stitch triangles to opposite sides of the square, matching the center creases. Stitch triangles to the remaining sides of the square to make the center unit. Trim the unit to measure 2½" square, including seam allowances.

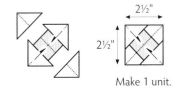

Make 1 unit.

2 Arrange the center unit, dark 1½" × 2½" rectangles, and light 1½" squares in three rows. Sew the pieces together into rows. Join the rows to make a Nine Patch Variation block measuring 4½" square, including seam allowances. Make a total of two blocks.

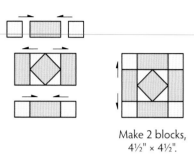

Make 2 blocks,
4½" × 4½".

Assembling the Quilt Top

1 Arrange the blocks and print 2½" × 4½" rectangles in five columns, referring to the quilt assembly diagram below and photo (page 49) for block placement.

2 Sew the blocks together into columns measuring 4½" × 24½", including seam

allowances. Join the columns, matching the seam intersections. The quilt top should measure 20½" × 24½".

Finishing the Quilt

For detailed information about any finishing steps, visit ShopMartingale.com/HowtoQuilt.

1 Layer the quilt top, flannel or batting, and backing; baste the layers together using your preferred method.

2 Quilt by hand or machine. Building Blocks is machine quilted in an allover small meander design.

3 Using the brown 1½"-wide strips, make single-fold binding (page 77) and then attach the binding to the quilt.

4 Make a label using a small piece of muslin, being sure to include your name and the date. Turn under the edges and hand stitch the label to the back of your quilt.

Quilt assembly

Temecula Treasures

PIECED AND HAND QUILTED BY SHERYL JOHNSON

The Capital T block appears in a variety of antique quilts. No Temecula Quilt Co. collection would be complete without at least a few—how about 20? These fabulous little blocks include a secret treasure: some very precious scraps from the first line of fabric I designed for Marcus Brothers. I will always cherish this Capital T quilt, a true Temecula Treasure. Whether you design yours in primary colors, gem tones, or pastels, it's sure to bring a smile.

Materials

Yardage is based on 42"-wide fabric.

1¼ yards total of assorted light, medium, and dark print scraps in red, blue, brown, cream, green, and gold for blocks

¼ yard of brown plaid for binding

⅝ yard of fabric for backing

22" × 26" piece of cream flannel or batting

"T" stands for **TEMECULA** *in my quilting universe. What does it stand for in yours?*

Cutting

For each block, select three prints with some contrast and label them prints A, B, and C. Two of the prints are for the center unit, and the third print is for the surrounding triangles. Use the quilt photo (page 53) for color inspiration when selecting pieces for the 20 blocks.

From print A, cut:

- 1 square, 3" × 3" (20 total)
- 2 squares, 2" × 2" (40 total)

From print B, cut:

- 1 square, 3" × 3" (20 total)
- 2 squares, 2" × 2" (40 total)

From print C, cut:

- 2 squares, 3¼" × 3¼"; cut the squares in half diagonally to yield 4 triangles (80 total)

From the brown plaid, cut:

- 3 strips, 1½" × 42" (60 total)

Making the Blocks

Press all seam allowances as indicated by the arrows.

1 Draw a diagonal line from corner to corner on the wrong side of the print A 3" square and layer it on top of the print B 3" square, right sides together. Sew ¼" from both sides of the drawn line. Cut on the line to yield two half-square-triangle units. Trim one unit to measure 2½" square and trim the remaining unit to measure 1½" square, including seam allowances. Repeat to make a total of 20 large and 20 small half-square-triangle units.

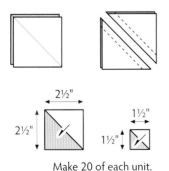

Make 20 of each unit.

2 Using print A and B 2" squares that match the units from step 1, repeat step 1 to make four half-square-triangle units. Trim each unit to measure 1½" square, including seam allowances. Repeat to make 80 small half-square-triangle units. Divide the units into 20 matching sets of five small units and one large unit.

Make 80 units.

3 Lay out one matching set of one large and five small half-square-triangle units, noting the orientation of the units. Sew the units together into rows. Join the rows to complete a center unit measuring 3½" square, including seam allowances. Make 20 units.

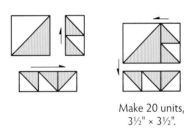

Make 20 units,
3½" × 3½".

4 Sew a print C triangle to one side of a center unit, lining up the triangle point with the center of the unit. Repeat on the opposite side of the unit. Add triangles to the remaining sides of the unit to make a Capital T block. Trim the block to measure 4¾" square, including seam allowances. Make 20 blocks.

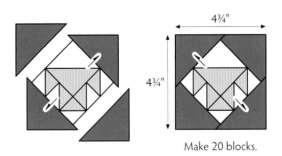

Make 20 blocks.

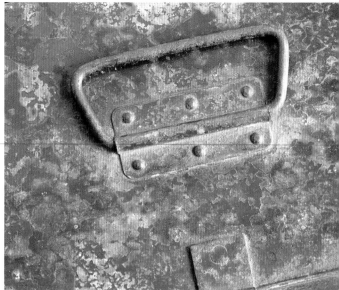

Assembling the Quilt Top

Arrange the blocks in five rows of four blocks each, referring to the quilt assembly diagram below. Sew the blocks together into rows. Join the rows, matching the seam intersections. The quilt top should measure 17½" × 21¾".

Quilt assembly

Finishing the Quilt

For detailed information about any finishing steps, visit ShopMartingale.com/HowtoQuilt.

1 Layer the quilt top, flannel or batting, and backing; baste the layers together using your preferred method.

2 Quilt by hand or machine. Temecula Treasures is hand quilted in a crosshatch pattern through the center of each block.

3 Using the brown plaid 1½"-wide strips, make single-fold binding (page 77) and then attach the binding to the quilt.

4 Make a label using a small piece of muslin, being sure to include your name and the date. Turn under the edges and hand stitch the label to the back of your quilt.

Lovely Ladders

PIECED BY SHERYL JOHNSON AND MACHINE QUILTED BY DEBBIE BLAIR

This quirky take on the traditional Jacob's Ladder block will let your favorite pink, tan, navy, and red scraps shine together like a tile mosaic. Some all-time favorites—Pinwheels, Half-Square Triangles, and Four Patches—are perfect for this design.

What's your favorite way of planning a color scheme? Do you lay out little bits of fabric on the bed? Are you a computer whiz with a program that does the hard work for you, or do colored pencils play a part? By paying careful attention to color placement, you'll create the fun, graphic center of Lovely Ladders.

Materials

Yardage is based on 42"-wide fabric.

⅛ yard of ivory print for blocks

¼ yard of red print for blocks and binding

¼ yard of navy print for blocks

¼ yard of gray print for blocks

⅓ yard of tan print for blocks

⅓ yard of pink print for blocks

⅔ yard of fabric for backing

23" × 31" piece of cream flannel or batting

Devote your attention to
COLOR AND FABRIC
*choice as you plan your
quilt layout.*

Cutting

From the ivory print, cut:

- 2 squares, 3" × 3"
- 36 squares, 1½" × 1½"

From the red print, cut:

- 7 squares, 3" × 3"
- 3 strips, 1½" × 42"
- 6 squares, 1½" × 1½"

From the navy print, cut:

- 12 squares, 3" × 3"
- 78 squares, 1½" × 1½"

From the gray print, cut:

- 4 squares, 3" × 3"
- 20 squares, 1½" × 1½"

From the tan print, cut:

- 13 squares, 3" × 3"
- 36 squares, 2" × 2"
- 42 squares, 1½" × 1½"

From the pink print, cut:

- 8 squares, 3" × 3"
- 36 squares, 2" × 2"
- 34 squares, 1½" × 1½"

Reposition Seams

When pressing four-patch units, or other block units, you can reduce bulk where the four seams meet. After the seam is sewn, use a seam ripper to remove the stitches above the crossed seam. Gently reposition the seam allowances to evenly distribute the fabric. Then press the seam allowances in opposite directions.

Making the Blocks

Press all seam allowances as indicated by the arrows.

1 Pair up the following 3" squares. For each pair of squares, draw a diagonal line from corner to corner on the wrong side of the lighter square.

- Two ivory and two navy squares
- Two red and two pink squares
- Four tan and four navy squares
- Four gray and four tan squares
- Six pink and six navy squares
- Five red and five tan squares

2 Starting with the pair of your choice, place the marked square on the unmarked square, right sides together. Sew ¼" from both sides of the drawn line. Cut on the line to yield two half-square-triangle units. Trim each unit to measure 2½" square, including seam allowances. Repeat with each pair to make the number of units indicated from each color combination (46 total). Set aside the red/tan units for assembling the bottom border.

2½"

2½"

Make 4 units.

Make 4 units.   Make 8 of each unit.

Make 12 units.   Make 10 units.

4 Referring to the photo on page 57 for color placement, lay out four half-square-triangle units and five four-patch units in three rows of three units each. Sew the units together in rows. Join the rows to make a Jacob's Ladder block measuring 6½" square, including seam allowances. Make nine blocks.

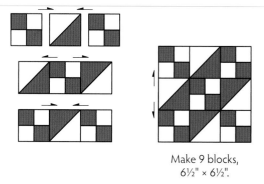

Make 9 blocks,
6½" × 6½".

3 Lay out two navy and two gray 1½" squares in two rows of two. Sew the squares together into rows. Join the rows to make a four-patch unit measuring 2½" square, including seam allowances. Repeat to make the number of units from each color combination as indicated in the diagram below (54 total). Set aside the navy/tan units for assembling the top border.

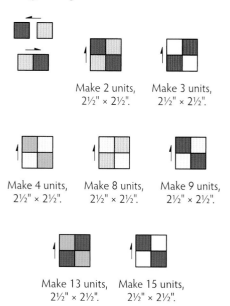

Make 2 units,
2½" × 2½".

Make 3 units,
2½" × 2½".

Make 4 units,
2½" × 2½".

Make 8 units,
2½" × 2½".

Make 9 units,
2½" × 2½".

Make 13 units,
2½" × 2½".

Make 15 units,
2½" × 2½".

Making the Borders

1 Join nine red/tan half-square-triangle units to make a strip measuring 2½" × 18½", including seam allowances. You'll have one red/tan unit left over for a future quirky quilt.

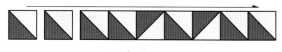

Make 1 strip,
2½" × 18½".

2 Join the navy/tan four-patch units to make a strip measuring 2½" × 18½", including seam allowances.

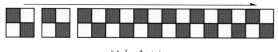

Make 1 strip,
2½" × 18½".

3 Draw a diagonal line from corner to corner on the wrong side of the tan 2" squares. Place a marked square on a pink 2" square, right sides together. Sew ¼" from both sides of the drawn line.

Cut on the line to yield two half-square-triangle units. Trim each unit to measure 1½" square, including seam allowances. Make 72 units.

Make 72 units.

4 Arrange the tan/pink half-square-triangle units in two rows of two, noting the orientation of each unit. Sew the units together into rows. Join the rows to make a Broken Dishes unit measuring 2½" square, including seam allowances. Make 18 units.

Make 18 units,
2½" × 2½".

5 Join nine Broken Dishes units, rotating every other unit 180° so seams abut. The strip should measure 2½" × 18½", including seam allowances. Repeat to make a second strip.

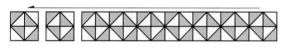

Make 2 strips,
2½" × 18½".

Assembling the Quilt Top

1 Lay out the Jacob's Ladder blocks in three rows of three blocks each, rotating the blocks as shown in the quilt assembly diagram at right. Sew the blocks together into rows. Join the rows, matching seam intersections. The quilt center should measure 18½" square, including seam allowances.

2 Sew the Broken Dishes strips to the top and bottom of the quilt center.

3 Sew the half-square-triangle strip to the bottom and the four-patch strip to the top of the quilt. The quilt top should measure 18½" × 26½".

Finishing the Quilt

For detailed information about any finishing steps, visit ShopMartingale.com/HowtoQuilt.

1 Layer the quilt top, flannel or batting, and backing; baste the layers together using your preferred method.

2 Quilt by hand or machine. Lovely Ladders is machine quilted in an allover small meander design.

3 Using the red 1½"-wide strips, make single-fold binding (page 77) and then attach the binding to the quilt.

4 Make a label using a small piece of muslin, being sure to include your name and the date. Turn under the edges and hand stitch the label to the back of your quilt.

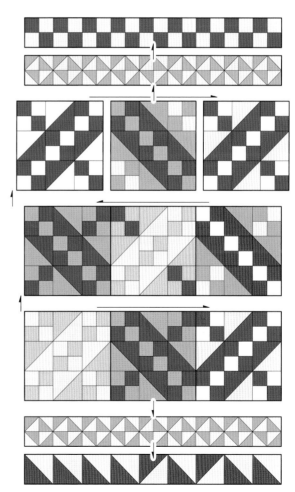

Quilt assembly

Patchwork Plates

PIECED BY SHERYL JOHNSON AND MACHINE QUILTED BY DEBBIE BLAIR

Sometimes it's all about the placement. The circa-1860 crib quilt that inspired Patchwork Plates was set with a soft pink fabric that made the scrappy Broken Dishes blocks shimmer and shine. Make your own version of this sweet little quilt with all the leftover pieces that fill your scrap basket. Carefully select light prints to create a little sparkle in each block and give this quilt the movement that will make it a vintage favorite. Here's one time when broken dishes are a joy.

Materials

Yardage is based on 42"-wide fabric.

1¼ yards *total* of assorted red, brown, black, gray, and gold prints for blocks (collectively referred to as "dark")

½ yard *total* of assorted cream and tan prints for blocks (collectively referred to as "light")

⅞ yard of pink print for setting squares

¼ yard of gray stripe for binding

2⅓ yards of fabric for backing*

42" × 49" piece of cream flannel or batting

If backing fabric is 42" wide after washing and trimming the selvages, you can use a single width of 1⅜ yards.

Cutting

From the dark prints, cut a total of:

- 180 squares, 2¾" × 2¾"

From the light prints, cut a total of:

- 60 squares, 2¾" × 2¾"

From the pink print, cut:

- 7 strips, 4" × 42"; crosscut into 60 squares, 4" × 4"

From the gray stripe, cut:

- 5 strips, 1½" × 42"

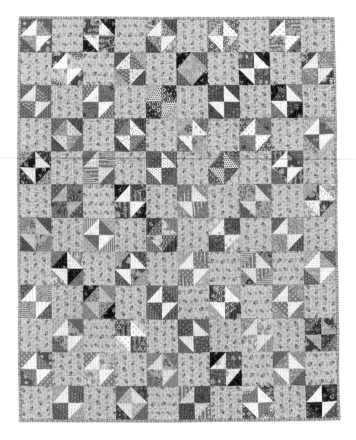

Think "sweet" and be **SELECTIVE** *when choosing fabrics for each Broken Dishes block. The lighter tone of the two interior triangles is what gives this quilt its shine.*

Making the Blocks

Press all seam allowances as indicated by the arrows.

1 Select two different dark 2¾" squares. Draw a diagonal line from corner to corner on the wrong side of the lighter square. Layer a marked square on an unmarked square, right sides together. Sew ¼" from both sides of the drawn line. Cut on the line to yield two half-square-triangle units. Trim each unit to measure 2¼" square, including seam allowances. Make 120 units.

Make 120 units.

2 Draw a diagonal line from corner to corner on the wrong side of the light squares. Layer a marked square on a dark square, right sides

together. Repeat step 1 to make 120 units measuring 2¼" square, including seam allowances.

Make 120 units.

3 Lay out two matching half-square-triangle units from step 1 and two matching units from step 2 in two rows of two. Sew the units together into rows. Join the rows to make a Broken Dishes block measuring 4" square, including seam allowances. Pay close attention to the position of the units, making sure to orient the light triangles toward the center of the block. Make 60 blocks.

Make 60 blocks, 4" × 4".

Assembling the Quilt Top

Lay out the blocks and the pink 4" squares in 12 rows, alternating them within each row and from row to row as shown in the quilt assembly diagram below. Sew the blocks and squares together into rows. Join the rows, matching seam intersections. The quilt top should measure 35½" × 42½".

Finishing the Quilt

For detailed information about any finishing steps, visit ShopMartingale.com/HowtoQuilt.

1 Layer the quilt top, flannel or batting, and backing; baste the layers together using your preferred method.

2 Quilt by hand or machine. Patchwork Plates is machine quilted in an allover feather design.

3 Using the gray striped 1½"-wide strips, make single-fold binding (page 77) and then attach the binding to the quilt.

4 Make a label using a small piece of muslin, being sure to include your name and the date. Turn under the edges and hand stitch the label to the back of your quilt.

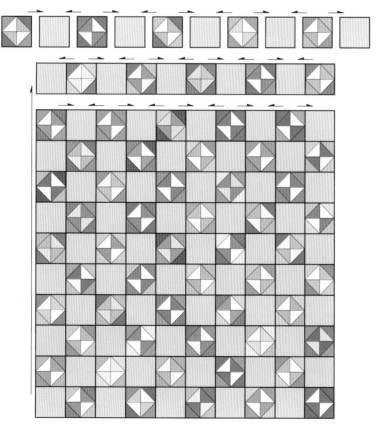

Quilt assembly

Butterfield Blues

PIECED AND HAND QUILTED BY SHERYL JOHNSON

Temecula Quilt Co. is located on Butterfield Stage Road in the beautiful Temecula Valley of California. In the mid-1800s, the Butterfield Overland Mail Company contracted with the federal government to deliver mail and goods to the area. Temecula was one of the stops along the Butterfield line. Wouldn't it be fun if a stagecoach, instead of a delivery truck, pulled up out front with a fresh supply of blue calicoes? For me, half the fun of quilting is creating contemporary pieces inspired by treasures from the past.

Materials

Yardage is based on 42"-wide fabric.

¼ yard of red print for blocks and binding

½ yard of ivory solid for blocks and border

¼ yard of cream print for blocks and border

½ yard *total* of assorted blue prints for blocks

¾ yard of fabric for backing

25" × 32" piece of cream flannel or batting

Cutting

From the red print, cut:

- 3 strips, 1½" × 42"
- 24 squares, 1" × 1"

From the ivory solid, cut:

- 1 strip, 3½" × 27½"
- 2 strips, 3½" × 14½"
- 8 strips, 1" × 42"

From the cream print, cut:

- 1 strip, 3½" × 27½"
- 2 strips, 1" × 42"

From the blue prints, cut a total of:

- 12 strips, 1" × 42"

Making the Blocks

Making the blocks in an assembly line is simpler than cutting the 1"-wide strips into the required lengths. Refer to the photo on page 68 for color placement as needed. When making the blocks, I randomly used cream strips instead of ivory strips. Press all seam allowances away from the center squares.

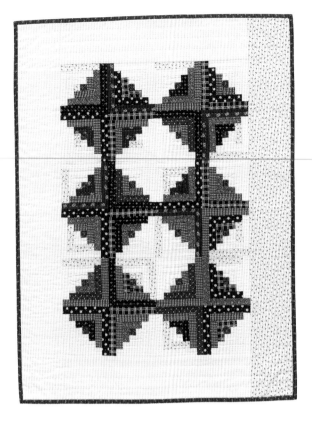

*Bring your past into the present by adding your own unique **TWIST** to a traditional quilt. Here, a bit of a print mixed in with ivory solid adds movement and interest to this little quilt.*

1 With right sides together, chain piece all 24 red squares to an ivory 1"-wide strip. Cut the units apart and press. Make 24 center units measuring 1" × 1½", including seam allowances.

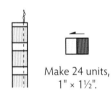

Make 24 units,
1" × 1½".

2 Stack the center units in a pile next to your machine with the red square at the bottom of the unit. Chain piece the units to an ivory 1"-wide strip, making sure the units are oriented with the red square at the bottom. Cut the units apart and press. Make 24 units measuring 1½" square, including seam allowances.

Make 24 units,
1½" × 1½".

3 In the same way, chain piece matching blue strips to the units from step 2, making sure to sew them to adjacent sides of the red square. Cut the units apart and press. Make 24 units measuring 2" square, including seam allowances.

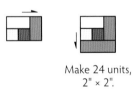

Make 24 units,
2" × 2".

4 Repeat steps 1–3 to sew ivory and then blue 1"-wide strips to the units from step 3. Make 24 units measuring 3" square, including seam allowances.

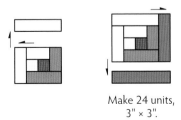

Make 24 units,
3" × 3".

5 Add a third round of ivory and blue 1"-wide strips to the units to make 24 blocks. The blocks should measure 4" square, including seam allowances.

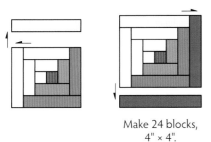

Make 24 blocks,
4" × 4".

Assembling the Quilt Top

1 Arrange the block in six rows of four blocks each, rotating the blocks in each row as shown in the quilt assembly diagram below. Sew the blocks together into rows. Join the rows, matching seam intersections. The quilt top should measure 14½" × 21½", including seam allowances.

2 Sew the short ivory strips to the top and bottom of the quilt top. Sew the long ivory strip to the left and the cream strip to the right side. The quilt top should measure 20½" × 27½".

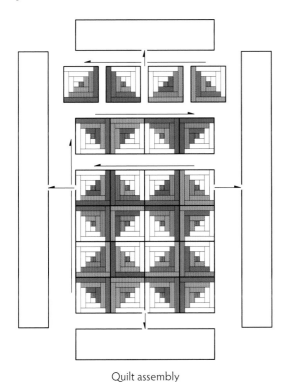

Quilt assembly

Finishing the Quilt

For detailed information about any finishing steps, visit ShopMartingale.com/HowtoQuilt.

1 Layer the quilt top, flannel or batting, and backing; baste the layers together using your preferred method.

2 Quilt by hand or machine. Butterfield Blues is hand quilted through the center of each log. Three lines, spaced 1" apart, are stitched throughout the border.

3 Using the red 1½"-wide strips, make single-fold binding (page 77) and then attach the binding to the quilt.

4 Make a label using a small piece of muslin, being sure to include your name and the date. Turn under the edges and hand stitch the label to the back of your quilt.

Little Leftovers

PIECED BY SHERYL JOHNSON AND MACHINE QUILTED BY DEBBIE BLAIR

An unknown quiltmaker's creation evolved from a variety of different blocks. She probably rummaged through the bottom of her sewing basket to rescue the remnants of yesteryear's projects. Perhaps she used a block from her daughter's doll quilt, then one from the wedding quilt she made for her brother and his bride. In the end, pieces of this and that from a variety of different projects converge to create a sampler with a collected-over-time twist. What long-lost memories does your sewing basket hold?

Materials

Yardage is based on 42"-wide fabric.

⅔ yard *total* of assorted red, blue, brown, black, green, gold, pink, and gray prints for blocks

⅓ yard of cream solid for quilt center and blocks

¼ yard of cream print for blocks

⅛ yard of blue check for blocks

⅛ yard of brown print for border

¼ yard of red plaid for binding

⅔ yard of fabric for backing

24" × 30" piece of cream flannel or batting

Cutting for Quilt Center

From the cream solid, cut:

- 6 squares, 3½" × 3½"; cut the squares into quarters diagonally to yield 24 side triangles
- 2 squares, 2⅛" × 2⅛"; cut the squares in half diagonally to yield 4 corner triangles
- 32 squares, 2" × 2"

From a variety of brown prints, cut:

- 36 squares, 2" × 2"

From the blue check, cut:

- 9 squares, 2" × 2"

Making the Quilt Center

Press all seam allowances as indicated by the arrows.

1 Referring to the quilt-center assembly diagram, lay out the cream solid, brown, and blue check squares in diagonal rows. Add the cream solid side triangles around the perimeter, omitting the corner triangles. Sew the pieces together into rows.

2 Join the rows, matching the seam intersections. Add the corner triangles last.

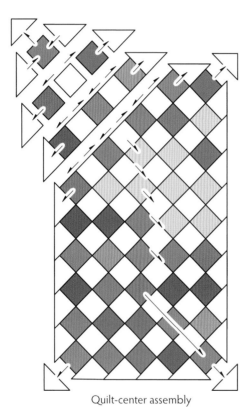

Quilt-center assembly

3 Square up the quilt center to measure 11" × 19½", making sure to leave ¼" beyond the points of all the squares for seam allowances.

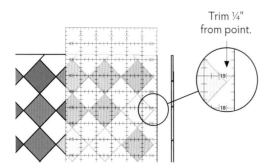

Trim ¼" from point.

Making the Blocks

For ease of following the instructions, the cutting and assembly are given individually for each type of block used in the border.

NINE PATCH

From a red print, cut:
- 5 squares, 2" × 2"

From a gold print, cut:
- 4 squares, 2" × 2"

Lay out the red and gold squares in three rows of three squares each. Sew the squares together into rows. Join the rows to make a Nine Patch block measuring 5" square, including seam allowances.

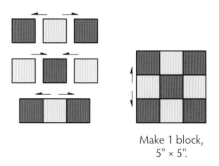

Make 1 block, 5" × 5".

HALF-SQUARE TRIANGLE

From a variety of brown and black prints, cut:
- 18 squares, 2½" × 2½"

From the cream print, cut:
- 14 squares, 2½" × 2½"

From the cream solid, cut:
- 4 squares, 2½" × 2½"

1 Draw a diagonal line from corner to corner on the wrong side of the cream squares. Layer a marked square on top of a brown or black square, right sides together. Sew ¼" from both sides of the drawn line. Cut the unit apart on the line to make two half-square-triangle units. Trim the units to measure 2" square, including seam allowances. Make 36 units.

Make 36 units.

2 Arrange nine half-square-triangle units in three rows of three units each. Sew the units together into rows. Join the rows to make a Half-Square Triangle block measuring 5" square, including seam allowances. Make four blocks.

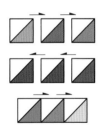

Make 4 blocks,
5" × 5".

FRIENDSHIP STAR

From a red print, cut:
- 2 squares, 2" × 2"
- 1 square, 1½" × 1½"

From the cream print, cut:
- 2 squares, 2" × 2"
- 4 squares, 1½" × 1½"

From a gold print, cut:
- 4 rectangles, 1¼" × 3½"

From a black print, cut:
- 4 squares, 1¼" × 1¼"

1 Draw a diagonal line from corner to corner on the wrong side of the cream 2" squares. Layer each marked square on top of a red 2" square, right sides together. Repeat step 1 of "Half-Square Triangle" (page 72) to make four half-square-triangle units. Trim the units to measure 1½" square, including seam allowances.

2 Lay out the half-square-triangle units, cream 1½" squares, and red 1½" square in three rows. Sew the units and squares together into rows. Join the rows to make a star unit measuring 3½" square, including seam allowances.

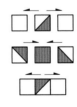

Make 1 unit,
3½" × 3½".

3 Sew gold rectangles to opposite sides of the star unit. Sew a black square to each end of the remaining gold rectangles. Sew the pieced strips to the top and bottom of the unit to make a Friendship Star block measuring 5" square, including seam allowances.

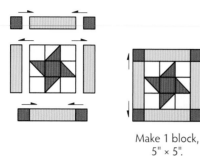

Make 1 block,
5" × 5".

IRISH CHAIN

From a pink print, cut:

- 8 squares, 1¼" × 1¼"

From a gray print, cut:

- 1 square, 2" × 2"

From the cream solid, cut:

- 4 rectangles, 1¼" × 3½"
- 4 rectangles, 1¼" × 2"

1 Sew four pink squares, the cream 1¼" × 2" rectangles, and the gray square together into three rows. Join the rows to make a center unit measuring 3½" square, including seam allowances.

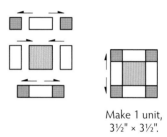

Make 1 unit,
3½" × 3½".

2 Sew four pink squares, the cream 1¼" × 3½" rectangles, and the center unit together into rows. Join the rows to make an Irish Chain block measuring 5" square, including seam allowances.

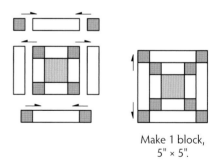

Make 1 block,
5" × 5".

Composed of leftover blocks, this **EXTRAORDINARY** *quilt has collected-over-time appeal.*

SQUARE-IN-A-SQUARE

From a red print, cut:

- 1 square, 2" × 2"

From the cream print, cut:

- 2 squares, 2¼" × 2¼"; cut the squares in half diagonally to yield 4 triangles

From a blue print, cut:

- 1 square, 3½" × 3½"; cut the square into quarters diagonally to yield 4 triangles

From a green print, cut:

- 2 squares, 3½" × 3½"; cut the squares in half diagonally to yield 4 triangles

1 Fold the red square in half vertically and horizontally, and lightly crease to mark the center on each side. Fold the cream print triangles in half, and lightly crease to mark the center of the long side. Sew triangles to opposite sides of the square, matching the center creases. Sew triangles to the remaining sides of the square to make a unit. Trim the unit to measure 2⅝" square, including seam allowances, making sure to leave ¼" beyond the points of the cream triangles for seam allowances.

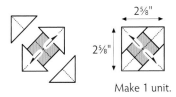

Make 1 unit.

2 Fold the blue triangles in half, and lightly crease to mark the center of the long side. Sew triangles to opposite sides of the unit, matching the center crease to the crossed seam. Sew triangles to the remaining sides of the square to make a unit. Trim the unit to measure 3⅝" square, including seam allowances.

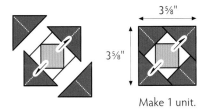

Make 1 unit.

3 Repeat step 2 using the green triangles to make the Square-in-a-Square block. Trim the block to measure 5" square, including seam allowances.

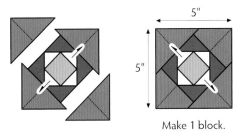

Make 1 block.

Making the Bottom Border

From a variety of assorted prints, cut:

- 11 squares, 2" × 2"
- 8 squares, 2½" × 2½"

From the cream print, cut:

- 5 squares, 2½" × 2½"

From the cream solid, cut:

- 3 squares, 2½" × 2½"

1 Draw a diagonal line from corner to corner on the wrong side of the cream squares. Layer a marked square on top of a print 2½" square, right sides together. Repeat step 1 of "Half-Square Triangle" (page 72) to make 16 half-square-triangle units. Trim the units to measure 2" square, including the seam allowances.

2 Join the half-square-triangle units and print 2" squares as shown to make the bottom border, which should measure 3½" × 20", including seam allowances. You'll have one half-square-triangle unit left over for a future quirky quilt.

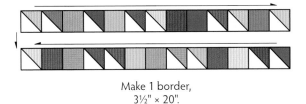

Make 1 border,
3½" × 20".

Assembling the Quilt Top

From the brown print for border, cut:

- 1 strip, 3½" × 20"

From the cream print, cut:

- 2 strips, 1" × 5"

From a gray print, cut:

- 2 strips, 1" × 5"

From the red plaid, cut:

- 3 strips, 1½" × 42"

1 Referring to the quilt assembly diagram below, join two Half-Square Triangle blocks, one cream strip, one gray strip, the Friendship Star block, and the Nine Patch block to make the left side border. Join two Half-Square Triangle blocks, one cream strip, one gray strip, the Square-in-a-Square block, and the Irish Chain block to make the right side border. Sew the borders to the left and right sides of the quilt center. The quilt center should measure 20" × 19½", including seam allowances.

2 Sew the half-square-triangle border to the bottom of the quilt. Sew the brown strip to the top of the quilt. The quilt top should measure 20" × 25½".

Finishing the Quilt

For detailed information about any finishing steps, visit ShopMartingale.com/HowtoQuilt.

1 Layer the quilt top, flannel or batting, and backing; baste the layers together using your preferred method.

2 Quilt by hand or machine. Little Leftovers is machine quilted in an allover small Baptist fan design.

3 Using the red plaid 1½"-wide strips, make single-fold binding (page 77) and then attach the binding to the quilt.

4 Make a label using a small piece of muslin, being sure to include your name and the date. Turn under the edges and hand stitch the label to the back of your quilt.

Quilt assembly

Single-Fold Binding

Most of the quiltmaking techniques I use will be familiar to quilters, but if you need help, go to ShopMartingale.com/HowtoQuilt for illustrated instructions on all sorts of quiltmaking topics. Where I do differ from many quiltmakers is in my binding. My quilts are small, so I prefer to use single-fold binding rather than the bulkier double-fold binding you might be familiar with. Here's how to make it.

1 Cut binding strips as directed in the project instructions. Using diagonal seams, sew the strips together to make a single long piece of binding.

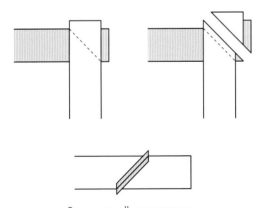

Press seam allowances open.

2 Turn under ¼" along one long raw edge of the binding and press.

3 Keeping right sides together and the raw edges aligned, place one end of the binding on the front of the quilt. Using a ¼" seam allowance, start stitching 4" to 5" from the end of the binding. When you approach a corner, stop ¼" from the edge, backstitch, and remove the quilt from the sewing machine.

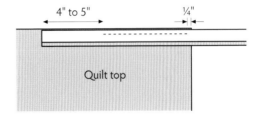

4 Fold up the binding at an angle, keeping the right edge of the binding aligned with the edge of the quilt.

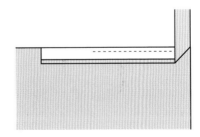

5 Fold the binding down as shown, keeping the top and side edges of the binding aligned with the edges of the quilt. Beginning with a backstitch, stitch the binding to the quilt. When you reach the next corner, backstitch ¼" from the edge, reposition the binding, and stitch the next side as before.

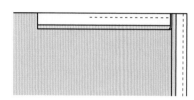

6 Continue stitching around the quilt until you're about 5" from the starting place. Remove the quilt from the sewing machine and then fold the ending strip up and the starting strip down, at a 90° angle, with the folds about ⅛" apart as shown. Finger-press the folds to crease.

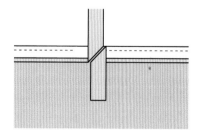

7 With right sides together, match the creases and pin. Sew along the crease, backstitching at each end and trimming to leave ¼" seam allowances. Press the seam allowances open. Realign the binding with the edge of the quilt and then stitch it in place.

8 Trim the batting and backing even with the edges of the quilt. Fold the binding to the back of the quilt, covering the binding stitches. Stitch the folded-under edge of the binding to the quilt by hand, sewing the folds of the mitered corners closed as you go.

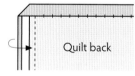

Quilt back

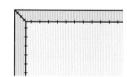